# Faith for the

## *Mompreneur*

NATASHA MILLER, MS, RHIA, CPC, CPC-I, CPB,
EDUCATOR, COACH, AUTHOR, SPEAKER

ISBN 978-0-692-09777-9

Printed in the United States of America

# CONTENTS

Dedication ....................................................... 5

Prayer of Salvation ........................................... 6

Foreword by Sheya Atterberry-Chisenga ............ 7

Preface ............................................................. 9

Introduction  Have Faith ................................... 13

Section 1:  Faith To Believe The Impossible ............. 19

Section 2:  Stepping Away From Corporate
America ............................................................ 29

Section 3:  Faith For The Mom ............................ 37

Section 4:  Faith For The Mompreneur ................. 43

Section 5:  Faith To Increase Finances/ Income ... 51

Section 6:  Faith To Build A Six Figure Income &
More .............................................................. 59

Section 7:  Faith For Balancing Your Life ............. 65

Mompreneur Faith Scriptures ........................... 85

Resources for Mompreneurs ............................... 99

Reference ....................................................... 101

# Dedication

I dedicate this book to my children: Jaron, Judah, Jadon, Jacqlyn, & Neema.  My children are the reason I am leaving a legacy. I pray that their faith moves mountains for them when they become adults.

I want to inspire moms, aunts, sisters, grandmas, and women all across the world to believe that with faith, they can do anything. I want to let others know that if God did it for me, he can do it for them.

# Prayer of Salvation

Lord Jesus, I believe you died for my sins.

Forgive me of my sins.

I believe you died and on the third day you rose.

Come into my heart, I confess you with my mouth that Jesus you are Lord and that God raised you from the dead!


If you prayed this prayer for the first time, you are saved! You are now able to walk out your faith life. Get into a bible-based church and keep God first in everything you do.

# Foreword by

# Sheya Atterberry-Chisenga

One of the most important attributes you must have as an entrepreneur is Faith. You must believe when you don't see or feel it. I am a Mompreneur and I adopted my niece, who lives in Zambia, Africa. The process to adopt a child internationally is very long, complicated, and expensive. I found myself starting to doubt, but what I love about this book is that it teaches you how to apply faith as a Mompreneur. Natasha uses real-life stories about how she applies faith in difficult circumstances and how God brought her family through.

As a mom who wishes to take control of her time and finances, and to offer her family a better life, Natasha shares stories, prayers, and scriptures to fuel your desire to move forward. This book is loaded with resources and tools you can use to take immediate action. Not only that, this book shows you how to write out your faith confessions, so you can start seeing the manifestation of what you are speaking over your life. Reading this book has reignited my faith to believe in the impossible. I know for sure that God will bring my daughter to America because I am a faith Mompreneur!

Sheya Atterberry-Chisenga

Business Coach, Speaker and Author

# Preface

*Faith for the Mompreneur* came about at the end of 2016, after I had written a story for the book *Stand Up Be Heard Volume 2*. The Lord spoke to me to write a book that would encourage moms who are business owners. The purpose of this book is to inspire moms and women all over the world, letting them know that with faith all things are possible. Faith should never be taken out of the equation. Often, we start strong with creating our businesses, then fall into a routine and forget what it took to get there. "Think of what he went through; how he put up with so much hatred from sinners! So do not let yourselves become discouraged and give up" (Hebrews 12:3 GNT). Even in writing this book, my faith was tested. I share in this book how I got pneumonia after having my baby girl. However, I never let my faith waiver. As Christians, we are not exempt from trials and tribulations. What counts is how we respond to them and whether we believe that we will overcome.

My husband and children have been instrumental to my writing this book. My mother was the first person to show me what an entrepreneur/Mompreneur was. When I was young, I did not quite understand the importance of owning a business, but now I do. Leaving a legacy is something my mother always shares with me and is why she started the businesses she did. I did not come from a silver spoon type of family, but I knew at an early age that I wanted to have the best. I wanted to own a home, I wanted to marry and have a family. Being a Mompreneur is more than having a flexible schedule and being able to work from home whenever I want. It is about leaving a legacy to my children and making a lasting impact on the world as a Christian.

While attending a women's conference, I heard a pastor say, "The Lord has been telling some of you to start your business." I remember this like it was yesterday. It happened five years ago, in November 2012, and that next month (December 2012), I had my business: Natasha Miller & Associates, LLC. I now have the DBA Northern California Medical Billing & Coding Institute (NCMBCI). In January 2013 I had my first class of students, filled to capacity - 10 students in a conference room! My faith allowed me to see it before it happened.

Natasha C. Miller

# Introduction

## Have Faith

Kingdom women of God, you have all been put here on assignment. Do not let your faith waiver! What are you believing in God for? As a wife, mom, grandma, sister, aunt, Mompreneur, or entrepreneur, what have you asked God to do? How do you know your faith is elevating?

I encourage you today to not give up and to not lose your faith. The bible says we need only the faith of a mustard seed! A mustard seed is very small to the naked eye. Start with mustard seed faith and then elevate your Faith. Do not expect God to be a microwave! Yes, you can experience some sudden miracles, but building your faith requires that you believe in and trust God!

I am reminded of Abraham, who wanted a son. Sarah was past the age of bearing children, but God spoke to Abraham, saying that Sarah would have a child even though she was over 100 years old. It took time for his manifestation to happen, but Abraham never doubted that it would.

After each chapter in this book, you will be able to start journaling your faith confessions and the dates. The journaling of your faith confessions will allow you to see how your faith grows and elevates. Begin to speak life over your faith confessions. The power of life and death is in your tongues. Be careful what you speak. If it doesn't align with the Word of God, do not speak it out of your mouth.

The first scripture I will share is Psalms 23. You may have learned this scripture as a child, but meditate on what it is saying.

Meditate on how you shall have no lack and no fear of evil with the Lord. Meditate on how the Lord has already prepared a table for you in the presence of your enemies.

## Psalms 23

**1** The Lord is my shepherd;

I shall not want.

**2** He makes me to lie down in green pastures;

He leads me beside the still waters.

**3** He restores my soul;

He leads me in the paths of righteousness

For His name's sake.

**4** Yea, though I walk through the valley of the shadow of death,

I will fear no evil;

For You are with me;

Your rod and Your staff, they comfort me.

**5** You prepare a table before me in the presence of my enemies;

You anoint my head with oil;

My cup runs over.

**6** Surely goodness and mercy shall follow me

All the days of my life;

And I will dwell[a] in the house of the Lord

Forever.

## PRAYER

Father God, I speak over every person reading this book, that their faith will be elevated to the next level. I pray that your faith moves and that you see the manifestations of your faith. Believe God and trust him! He loves you and wants the best for you! In Jesus' Name. Amen.

# Section 1:

# Faith to Believe the Impossible

My journey toward believing the impossible. I had given birth to three boys and always wanted a girl. Of course everything happens in God's timing. On August 2, 2017 at 11:56 pm, my faith baby was born. I gave birth to Neema Faith Miller, an 8-pound, 13.6-ounce healthy baby girl.

As I mentioned, I had always wanted to have a baby girl. Before Neema arrived, I had two miscarriages. Going to the doctor and having the doctor say "I am sorry, I do not hear and see a heartbeat" was devastating. It was one of the worst feelings I'd ever had. I started to doubt God. I started to believe that something was wrong with me. I could not understand why this was happening. I knew deep down that I wanted another child, but I wanted to have a girl.

During this time of healing, I had to build up my Faith. One thing I know about God is that he will give you the desires of your heart if you keep him first. Of course, I had my own personal deadline for having children. I told myself that if I did not get pregnant by age 30, I was done having children.

I was 34, past my personal deadline. At the end of 2016, I finally told myself that if I did not get pregnant by the end of the year, I was not going to try anymore. I did not know that I was already pregnant. One thing I had to realize was that you cannot set deadlines on God's time. The scripture says, in Jeremiah 29:11: "For I know the plans I have for you,' declares the Lord, 'plans to prosper you and not to harm you, plans to give you hope and a future.'"

Birthing my faith baby elevated my faith to the next level!

Getting pregnant one last time took Faith! I was always asked when I was going to have more children, whether I would try for a baby girl. My response was never no. It was always "Oh, I don't know, we will see!" In my mind, I knew I wanted to have a girl.

My husband and I would talk about having another. After I finished my master's degree program, I knew I wanted to try for my girl and I knew my faith was going to let it to happen. Eight years later, after I had my last son, my baby girl came.

Sometimes we are so quick to rush God and to rush the process or outcome, but that is not Faith!

## In the Delivery Room

Even in the delivery room, I had to use my faith. The doctor was threatening a C-section. My baby's heart rate kept dropping every time I had a contraction. I was praying, and so was my husband. I said to the Lord, "With all my children, you brought me too far without a C-section to have one now." Next thing I knew, the doctor said I was fully dilated and it was time to push. We were all surprised – even the nurses – because it went really quickly. I pushed for only 10 minutes and there was Neema: a healthy 8-pound baby girl! I believed a God for a girl and he blessed me and my family with one. I did not try any gimmicks or tricks; I just trusted God.

(Neema Faith Born)

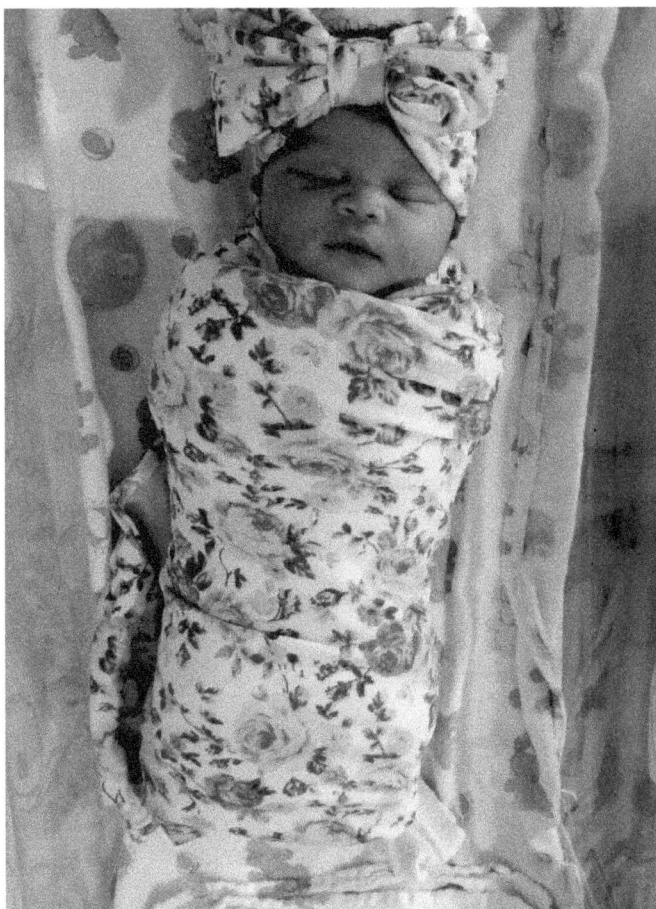

### Faith to Believe

Your faith cannot be shaken. You cannot doubt when it seems as though things are moving too slowly. What are you believing God for today? What has God done for you in the past? I put my faith and trust in God. I believe wholeheartedly that what I ask for will happen. God wants to know that you are all in. With what is going on in the world, you might start to doubt God, but you must stay focused on Him. The bible says, "But without faith it is impossible to please Him, for he who comes to God must believe that He is, and that He is a rewarder of those who diligently seek Him" (NKJV). Our entire disposition must be built on Faith!

## PRAYER

I speak and pray over everyone, that you have crazy Faith! I pray that you have faith to believe the impossible. I speak that your faith pleases God and he moves on your behalf. I speak and pray over every woman who has been trying to get pregnant or who has had miscarriages, that your womb is healed In Jesus' Name! Amen!

## FAITH CONFESSIONS

Write down your Faith Confessions
pertaining to Believe.

| Faith Confession | Date | Date Manifested |
|---|---|---|
|  |  |  |
|  |  |  |
|  |  |  |

# Section 2:

# Stepping Away From Corporate America

Balancing the roles of wife, mom, and entrepreneur is never easy.

That is why I decided to leave the corporate world. I found that I spent less of my time and days with my children. My days started before the sun came up and ended after the sun went down – many days outside my house. I found myself married with four children to whom I was unavailable. I was so tired from working and commuting to work that I did not have the energy to do anything when I came home. Sometimes my commute to work was one to two hours each way. I am sure you, as a mom, are reading this book and finding it hard to make time for yourself, your spouse, and your children. I realized that if I could commute, travel, and not get much in return, I could put all that time and energy into my own business so that I could have time for my family. I realized that all I needed was Faith! Faith allowed me to step away completely from my corporate job and to work fully on my business. Balancing the roles of mom and business owner is key. Structure must be in place to ensure that you do not overwhelm yourself. That means setting your schedule and making your calendar work for you. Block out time to work on your business and then block out time for yourself and your family. If you are working from home, that can become tricky, but you must set aside hours for yourself just like if you were going to an office. Of course, you have the benefit of being able to rearrange your time, but try to stick to your calendar so that you are not all over the place.

If stepping away from corporate America is your goal, start today to make your dream a reality. Hiring a life coach like me would be a great start, but if you are not ready for a life coach, you can start with what you have. List what you would like to do, find out whether you have the skills you need or whether you must acquire them, start your research, write down your goals and the dates by which you would like to accomplish them. I would also add that you should find a mentor, someone who is working from home or who is an entrepreneur. Please do not mistake a mentor for a coach, as they are two different things. I have both a mentor and a coach. When I started my business, I had only a mentor. My mentor showed me how to start my business and allowed me to help with her business. Pray that God sends you the mentor who is right for you and your business.

When I stepped away from corporate America, I did not simply wake up and say, "Today is my last day." I put a plan in place and worked that plan. Your plan can consist of, for example, working on your business every day for two hours while you are still working your day job. Working on your plan is important because, remember, faith without works is dead! I worked in corporate America when I started my business. As an entrepreneur, you must always remember your why: why you decided to become an entrepreneur.

Writing out your why and framing it so that you see it every day could help you on days when things do not seem to be going the way you want them to go.

God wants us to have more than enough. He wants to use your gifts in the marketplace to help someone else. If you know deep down inside that you are not fulfilling your purpose and what God has called you to do, you must take action now. Get around like-minded people who are going - or who are already - where you want to be. Do not make things harder than they must be. Do your research and start to take action today. Many people know that they are supposed to be doing something different or more, but they just sit on it. The worst thing you can do is let fear paralyze you. Take action today!

## PRAYER

I speak and pray over every woman who wants to step away from corporate America and start her own business. Father, I pray that you stir up the gifts in them and that they move forcefully and boldly in what you have called them to do. I pray that they begin to plan and take action. I pray that their businesses are successful and that they reach the people whose problems you have been waiting for them to solve. In Jesus' Name. Amen.

## FAITH CONFESSIONS

Write down your Faith Confessions pertaining to your Career or Entrepreneurship.

| Faith Confession | Date | Date Manifested |
|---|---|---|
|  |  |  |
|  |  |  |
|  |  |  |

# Section 3:

# Faith for the Mom

As women, we face a lot on a daily basis. For wives and moms, the responsibilities are greater. Before we were created in our mothers' wombs, God knew what we would face and what would challenge us.

It has not always been easy for me as a wife, mom, and entrepreneur. One thing I can say is that when I completed one hard task, I learned that I am not easily broken and that I can do more. Quitting has never been an option for me.

Do not get me wrong; sometimes you must slow down and rest. The devil really tried to discourage me after I had my baby girl. I ended up in the emergency room two times back to back with complications and pneumonia. Having pneumonia was not a great feeling, but one thing I said on a daily basis was that I was healed. I spoke over myself healing and read healing scriptures. I aligned my faith with the Word of God. I am healed and back to doing what God has called me to do!

The enemy is on his job every day and does not miss a beat. We must ensure we are on our job! Going through that sickness restored and strengthened my Faith. The illness showed me the importance of rest! As women and moms, we must take time to rest and take care of ourselves, especially after having a baby.

My father has passed away, but one thing he always told me is to ensure I get my rest. Now I understand even more what he was telling me. Moms, we must take time out and do something nice for ourselves. We can get so busy taking care of everyone else and running our businesses that we forget to take care of ourselves. Take time out for yourself at least once a month. You can pamper yourself, read a book, or take a short trip. Do something for yourself.  One thing is for sure: time will keep moving and you do not want to look up 10 years from now and be tired and exhausted, having done nothing for yourself.

Have the faith to believe God will keep your children.  As moms, we all want the best for our children, but we must have faith that if our children are not walking in Christ, they will return to Him.  As moms, we train our children every day, showing them what to do and what not to do. My children will be grown one day and I pray for them on a continual basis, that the Lord keeps them and that they find out at an early age their life purpose. I also give them guidance based on the gifts and talents that God has given them.  The world is so evil and it is our responsibility as moms to nurture and guide our children with Christian principles.

## PRAYER

I pray that every mom begins to have a spiritual discernment on how to balance her life as a mom. I pray that every mom begins to find time to rest and enjoy the small and big moments. I speak over every mom to find it a joy to be a mom to their children and that God gives them the strength to train their children in the way they should go. I pray over all moms' children, that the Lord keeps them safe from hurt, harm, and danger. I speak life over all moms reading this prayer, that they begin to speak life, encouragement, and wisdom to their children. In Jesus' Name. Amen.

## Faith Confessions

Write down your Faith Confessions pertaining to you being a Mom, Grandma, Sister, and Friend.

| Faith Confession | Date | Date Manifested |
|---|---|---|
|  |  |  |
|  |  |  |
|  |  |  |

# Section 4:

# Faith for the Mompreneur

Being a Medical Mompreneur is not just about me; it is about preparing my children to learn how they can become business owners and have wealth. During many of our conversations, we talk about where they see themselves in the future and how to build wealth.

Running a business is not for the weak. It takes work and dedication. It takes getting some no's. However, the rewards are exceptional! You have your own business. You have more time with your family. You can watch your children participate in sports or extracurricular activities. You can drop off and pick up your children from school. Ultimately, you have the freedom and flexibility to create your own schedule.

You have the opportunity to make unlimited income. Ask yourself how much you want to make on a monthly or yearly basis. From there, begin to use your Faith. You cannot use your faith if you do not put it to something.

Take the time now to determine how much you want to make and write it down.

Monthly

_____

Yearly

_____

**Faith to Build Your Team.** Having your own business and family will eventually require you to build a team. You cannot be afraid to upgrade and add individuals to your business. Adding people to your team does not necessarily have to cost a lot of money up front. One thing you can do to build your team is to hire freelancers or contractors to work on certain projects. You can hire a virtual assistant to help with administrative work, which can free up your time to concentrate more on your business. You can also hire an intern to help with marketing. Now, more than ever, is a great time to be in business. With social media and the Internet, you can reach so many people, which gives you the ability to grow your business more than ever before.

Mompreneur, do not give up on your Faith. You cannot quit! You have a special calling on you and your family, and the world is waiting for you to completely show up. Not completely showing up is not an option. Being lazy is not an option. If you become tired during your journey, get back to the basics. Keep God first in everything you do. Also remember to ask for help when you need it. It never does a person good to not ask for help.

Did you know that in the United States we have "11.3 million woman-owned businesses" and that the highest "percentage of woman-owned firms" is in the field of healthcare (64%) (Score, 2016)?

Wow, women, we are something else. We are helping create revenue and jobs! Do not give up on yourself. If you must re-evaluate and make some changes, do so, but know that you are wanted and needed in the marketplace.

The infographic below shows how women in business are making a significant difference.

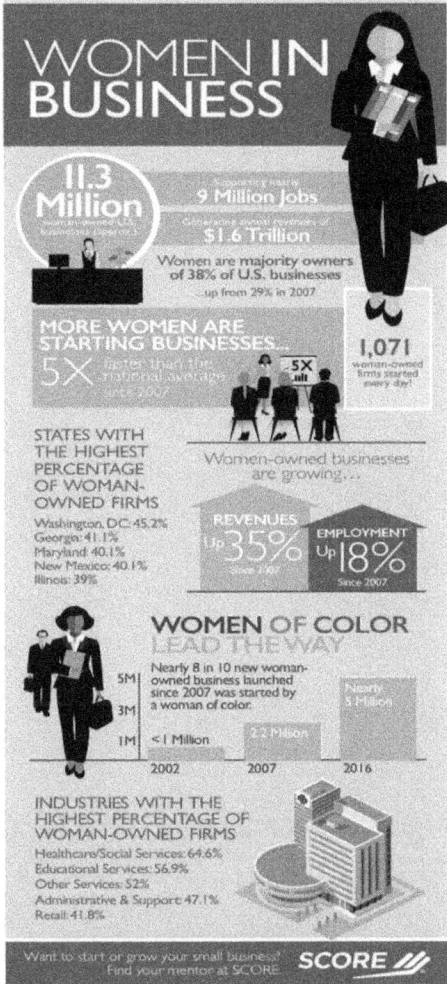

Mompreneur, you must have a personal mission statement so that you stay focused and know your "what" and "why." Take some time to dig deep and write out your personal mission statement. One thing about your statement is that it can always be updated. Refer back to your statement once a month to ensure you are on track.

Personal Mission Statement

_____

_____

_____

_____

## PRAYER

Father God, I pray that you stir up the
gifts in everyone reading this book! I pray
that you show them new ideas and how to
build their team successfully. I pray that
they have nothing lacking and that whatever
they put their hands to do prospers. I pray
that you continue to show them how to be a
Mompreneur or business owner and that
new clients and opportunities come their
way. In Jesus' Name. Amen.

## FAITH CONFESSIONS

Write down your Faith Confessions for the Mompreneur.

| Faith Confession | Date | Date Manifested |
|---|---|---|
|  |  |  |
|  |  |  |
|  |  |  |

# Section 5:

# Faith to Increase
# Finances/Income

There was a time in my life when my faith had not met up with my finances. For a short time, my husband and I had to receive food stamps because our income was so low. We had a total of four children combined, and three of our children were with us full time living in a two-bedroom apartment. I knew our situation was temporary. We were also receiving WIC, which helped provide formula and other items for my children. Now, I do not have a problem with these resources; I just knew I did not want the assistance at all, nor did I want it for a long time. During those periods, I knew I had to use my faith more. The scriptures say, "For I say, through the grace given to me, to everyone who is among you, not to think *of* himself more highly than he ought to think, but to think soberly, as God has dealt to each one a **measure of faith**" (NKJV, Romans 12:3).

I began using my Faith, and before I knew it, opportunities arrived. I took a risk and left my state job, which was not paying much at all, and accepted a temporary position. Sometimes elevating your faith can seem like taking a risk. As a result of my Faith, another opportunity opened up, which started the process of increasing my income. As a mom, I wanted the best for my children, so I sacrificed commuting on a daily basis so that I could provide more for them.

Now my faith was working and I continued to encourage and support my husband in finding work that provided more income. I could not see what was working behind the scenes, but I knew something was going to change for our family. On a daily basis, I was his cheerleader and shared with him that he was to use his Faith. My husband got the call for the full-time permanent position he wanted. God positioned it so that his pay and benefits were great.

Our family is also a giving family and we believe in the sowing and reaping principle. The scripture says, "But this I say: He who sows sparingly will also reap sparingly, and he who sows bountifully will also reap bountifully" (NKJV, 2 Corinthians 9:6). Years ago, we decided to give a $1,000 seed offering above our normal tithe and offering. Once we did that, our finances never lacked. I put a name to our seed offering, and that was to buy a house. With that seed offering, we were able to buy our first home. I did not worry about how much money we had in the bank. I did not worry about how much the down payment and closing cost would be. I just knew it was time to buy a house. I knew that my faith was going to allow us to get there. It did not take long, either! God moved expediently and our cost to move into our house was less than $2,000. Due to our Faith, we are homeowners and have paid off a large amount of debt.

Continue using your faith pertaining to your finances and income. The bible says we are to be lenders and not borrowers. God can position the right people to come into your life. All it takes is for one person to send you unlimited referrals to boost your business. Believe God, that if he told you to start your business, he will not leave you dissolute. Be a good and faithful steward of your finances. Set a budget and, if you are married, communicate with your husband about your family's financial goals. You should not be in the same spot year after year. If you did not grow up with an upbringing of financial literacy, you have the power and authority to change that. Take some classes, upgrade your life so that you can begin to see the increase.

When my husband and I were in the beginning of our marriage, we used the envelope system. I would take the cash out of the bank after getting paid and put our money in designated envelopes. Doing that allowed us to spend wisely and pay off debt. You can become disciplined in your finances if you believe and do the necessary work.

## PRAYER

Father God, I speak over everyone's finances and income to increase. Your word says that you give us the power to get wealth. I pray that you give us the resources, skills, and ability to run our businesses successfully. I pray that God sends you new clients, new business opportunities, and money to further grow our businesses. I pray favor to allow us all to go into the marketplace to achieve the wealth you have stored up for us. In Jesus' Name! Amen!

## FAITH CONFESSIONS

Write down your Faith Confessions pertaining to your Finances/Income.

| Faith Confession | Date | Date Manifested |
|---|---|---|
|  |  |  |
|  |  |  |
|  |  |  |

# Section 6:

## Faith to Build a Six-Figure Income & More

Often, people are not making the bare minimum of what they are worth because they do not think they deserve it. Who told you that you could make only so much? Was it your parents, your manager, yourself? For an entrepreneur, having multiple streams of income is a plus, but you do not necessarily have to be stretched out to make six figures.

Building your business takes faith and building your income takes a team. To see an overflow of abundance, you must begin building a team. This does not mean you must get brick and mortar, but you must learn how to delegate.

One thing I have learned to do is delegate my tasks and projects. I can accomplish more when I have a person or two helping me behind the scenes. You can start small with a virtual assistant (VA). Having a virtual assistant has been a huge blessing for me and my business. I have been able to focus more on content, for example, while having my VA work on administrative and social media tasks. You must get away from the mindset that you can do it all and still see financial growth.

Partnering is another option that might be beneficial. You must ensure that you have a solid agreement in place. It is also important that all partners involved have a clear understanding of their roles and responsibilities.

Speaking is one way to increase your income. A few years ago, the healthcare industry was preparing for the transition of ICD-9 codes to ICD-10 codes. As an expert in my industry, I was paid to travel, speak, and train providers, nurses, medical coders, and medical billers on how to properly use the new ICD-10 code sets. Speaking also allows you to market yourself.

Becoming an author provides you with an opportunity to not only say that you are an author, but to share with the world what God has given you to share. Writing and selling books will never get old. We all had to learn how to write and speak; instructions, directions, and guidance all come in the form of some type of manual or book. Even the bible was written, and it is read every day.

Selling products in addition to a service is another way to boost your income. As an entrepreneur, you should always have products to sell. Through my business, I teach classroom and online courses. The online courses seem to be what more of my customers are wanting. Creating a course on a learning management system is not as hard as you may think it is. Selling digital products or e-books is always great, too.

## PRAYER

Father God, I pray that you give the women reading this book double for their trouble. I pray that you increase their finances and income, for your word says that you will faithfully reward them. I pray that you give every person reading this book the sincerity to have more faith to achieve the desires of their hearts, to be able to receive six figures and more, to continue establishing your covenant. In Jesus' Name! Amen!

## FAITH CONFESSIONS

Write down your Faith Confessions
pertaining to faith to Build a Six-Figure
Income & More.

| Faith Confession | Date | Date Manifested |
|---|---|---|
|  |  |  |
|  |  |  |
|  |  |  |

# Section 7:

# Faith for Balancing Your Life

Yes, the scripture says, "faith without works is dead." As moms, Mompreneurs, or women in general, we must be able to balance our lives. If you do not take care of yourself, how will you be able to take care of anyone else?

First, I want to start with the spiritual aspect. It is important to take time out to pray and meditate on what God wants you to do. Starting your mornings with prayer, before you do anything else, is the primary way to balance out your everyday and your entire life. Praying and reading God's word will help you stay balanced in every area of your life.

Next is to take care of yourself. Once you have begun taking care of your life's spiritual aspects, you will be able to more easily balance your life as a mom, Mompreneur, or woman. Then you want to take care of yourself so that you have the energy to take care of your family and those in need - those waiting for you in the marketplace. In taking care of yourself, you want to do something for yourself at least once a month. It does not have to be expensive. It can be having coffee with a friend or two. It can be going to the movies. It can be buying yourself something inexpensive. I take care of myself by getting massages. I like to get massages; it helps relieve stress and tension. I also like to get pedicures and manicures. That helps me keep together my physical appearance and continue pampering myself.

Once I am taken care of, I am available to take care of my husband and children. I am available to go out into the community and have more clarity on what it is that God has called me to do. Maybe going to a women's retreat once a year can help you stay balanced. Some people take a relaxing day and do nothing. We are all human and we must all rest to rejuvenate ourselves so that we can be our best. There's nothing wrong with taking a day just for yourself to relax and do nothing, turning off everything to ensure that you are able to hear from God and continue the assignment he has called you to do.

Another aspect is making sure you are eating and preparing healthy meals. My family is large. I have a husband and five children, so we try to use our Crock-Pot as much as possible. We also try to overnight our meat so that if anything must be seasoned, it is ready to go for the next day. Having a fresh butter lettuce salad is one way to eat a healthy meal; you can add vegetables or fruits according to your taste. Baked fish and baked chicken are also healthy meals. Try to prepare your meals ahead of time, especially if you are working outside the house. Even if you are working in the house, regardless of whether you have children, eating healthy meals will help you fulfill the destiny to which God has called you. I see so many people who suffer from chronic conditions that can be controlled or eliminated by consuming healthier foods. We must recognize this and take control of our lives, refraining from consuming fast food that is not good for us. We need the God-given faith to take control and eat healthier. This is one way to maintain balance in your life.

The next thing I will suggest that moms, Mompreneurs, or women do is create a schedule. I have calendars; I love them. I use my phone as a calendar but I also have a passion planner. With a passion planner, you can create a schedule for the whole year. It includes a slot for every time of the day (though, no, you do not have to fill out each of those slots). The ability to write things down, have clarity, and focus on what you must do for the day, the week, or the month will help you balance your life. Listing your top three priorities is another way to balance your life – and not just your work life but your personal life as well. We want to ensure that we are taking care of our families and our homes. Communicate your schedule to your husband and children because it's not about just you. You must ensure that everyone knows what is going on. Maybe you can have a short meeting every week to discuss what must get done for the household. That can help create balance;

you will not feel as though everything is on your plate.  My husband and I work together as a team; it is very important that we create a schedule and that everyone takes part in it.

You shouldn't feel like you are doing everything because then you will feel overwhelmed. If you are overwhelmed, you are not operating in the Spirit of the Lord.

Another way to have faith to balance your life involves your business.  If you are an entrepreneur, a Mompreneur, or a business woman, you want to ensure that, in everything, you have what I call a Mompreneur suit.  You want to have at least one nice suit and one nice white blouse.  In addition, you want to ensure that you have the 4 Gs: looking great, feeling great, smelling great, and thinking great.  In all respects, the Mompreneur suit allows you to go out into the marketplace and serve your people in a professional way. If you have only one suit to start out with, work on building up your closet from there. This would be a great thing to do.

Having faith to balance your life will take organization. The scripture tells us, in 1 Corinthians 14:40 NIV Version, "But everything should be done in a fitting and orderly way." To have balance in our lives, we must be organized. What does that look like? We need a system in place for our households and our businesses. You must be able to prioritize what needs to get done. How can you do this? Create your three must-DOs for the day, for the week, and for the month, then prioritize those using the passion planner I mentioned previously. If there's a section to do so, write down what you want to focus on for today. You'll have one, two, or three things. List your top three priorities, what you must get done.

Here is another way to stay organized. Like I said, I have a large family, and I have folders in place for all my kids, as well as for me and my husband. Anything that comes in - schoolwork, important papers, mail - goes into each person's folder. We make sure to throw out or shred anything we no longer need so we're not constantly taking in and keeping paperwork.

Another way to become organized - and what I have done in my house - is to start with one simple, small project in one room and then move on to the next. For example, to organize my closets, I bought portable baskets on Amazon. You can write out labels and put them inside the baskets. I use them to organize my entire closet. Using those baskets and labels, I created a system for where everything goes - dry towels, large towels, hand towels, sheets, children's sheets, etc. I ensure that everything matches up accordingly. This is one way to establish organization in a closet. Before I had that system in place, I had sections, like one row for different items, but it never looked neat. Things were thrown in and when someone opened the closet, towels or sheets could easily fall out because my children were not putting in the items correctly. Now we have our system in place, and it is so much better.

Another thing I recently did to organize my house involved my kitchen pantry. I ordered some small unit shelves through Amazon. Using them, I have been able to organize my pantry. Everything in my kitchen - canned goods, snacks, paper goods, breakfast items, pasta - is now completely organized. It's easy to see if something is missing, or if we need to put something on the grocery list. Things are not just thrown in the pantry. The pantry is organized and creates less anxiety for me as a mom. In addition, if a guest comes over, they can open up the pantry and be able to help themselves.

Those are just some simple ways to get organized. You can also hire someone to help you clean your house. I myself do this to keep my life balanced. Having someone come over to clean my house allows me to live in an orderly fashion. If I decide to have company at the last minute, I feel comfortable because I know my house is organized. If your budget does not permit you to hire a cleaner, simply ensure that you have a system in place. If you have children, they must have chores. We do this in my house; even though someone comes in to clean, my children all have tasks to complete themselves. You can also keep your house clean and organized by ensuring that you do not have too much on your plate, which will give you time to perform these tasks.

It's very important to be organized not just in your personal life but in your business life. Have faith and believe that God will send people to help you become organized, especially if you lack in those skills. Ask God to lead you to the people who can help you organize your business and your policies and procedures. Have those in place. Organize your office, whether it is outside or inside your home. It is hard to work and have clarity if you are not organized. It's hard to have a vision or to go forth on your mission if you do not have organization in place. If you are lacking in organization, I encourage you to ask the Lord to show you who can help you in this respect or how you can do it yourself. When you become organized, you are able to fully walk out and do more, to be more productive in your day, in your week, in your month, and in your year.

In this book, you will find a worksheet. I want you to start taking better care of yourself. I want you to write down what you can start doing once a month. You will see a section about what you can do for yourself at least once a quarter. Then write down what you can do for yourself once a year. Use this worksheet; if you think of new ideas, return to the worksheet and list them there. However, don't just write things down. Faith without works is dead. I want you to take care of yourself and do what is on your paper.

Also, in this book you will find a worksheet on "How to Balance Life as a

Woman and Mom." What are some things you can start doing right now to balance your life? In each section, I want you to write down two or three things you can do now or that you would like to do. Each section will follow what is in the book. So, for healthy meals, you will see a worksheet that aligns with that section in this book. For spiritual matters, write down three things you can do to improve yourself. In taking care of yourself, what can you do right now to balance your life? For a Mompreneur suit or signature suit, write down three different suits that you would like. Research where you can find these suits and price them out. Also, write down when you will be able to see yourself obtaining these suits and putting them into your closet. For your schedule, in terms of balancing your life, write down right now what you can do, what you are doing, or what you can do differently in terms of scheduling. Stick to your schedule as much as possible and be organized. I want you to write down three things you can do to balance your life in terms of organization in your house, in your office, on your job, with your children, with your husband, and so forth. These are just some of the principles for balancing your life.

## Prayer

Father God, I pray that you give everyone reading this book the strategies, tools, and resources to balance their lives and live for you. I pray that your will is done in our lives and that we submit totally to you. I pray that our lives are free from too much activity and that we are open to hearing from you. I pray that you allow us to stay focused and clear on what you have called us to do. I pray that you give us the strength to do all that you have called us to do. In Jesus' Name! Amen!

## FAITH CONFESSIONS

Write down your Faith Confessions
pertaining to Balancing Your Life.

| Faith Confession | Date | Date Manifested |
|---|---|---|
|  |  |  |
|  |  |  |
|  |  |  |

# Conclusion

I hope this book provides you with resources, tools, and strategies for moving forward with your Faith. Building your faith is like building your muscles; it takes time for the muscles to show, but eventually they will show, due to your continual efforts. It is the same with your Faith. You can have what you say, but it will take work. It is time to take your faith to the next level.  The time is now for you to start your business, advance in your income, and leave a legacy to your children and family.   Remember that only what you do for Christ will last.

Become Kingdom-minded and watch God move on your behalf in your family and business.

Continue trusting in God and believe and remember that faith without works is dead! Let's get to work on our Faith Confessions so we can edify the body of Christ and help restore our children, families, and communities.

# How to Balance Life as a Woman/Mom

What are some things you can do to balance your life? In each section, write down two or three things that you do now or that you want to do to balance and improve your life.

Healthy Meals

1.

2.

3.

Spiritual

1.

2.

3.

## Take Care of Yourself

1.

2.

3.

## Mompreneur Suit/Signature Suit

1.

2.

3.

## Schedule

1.

2.

3.

## Be Organized

1.

2.

3.

# Mompreneur Faith Scriptures

In this section I provide some of my favorite scriptures that have helped me keep and elevate my Faith. Read and meditate on these scriptures, especially when you feel like you are losing faith in any aspect of your life. I pray that your faith is elevated and that you continue seeing with your spiritual eyes.

**Hebrews 11:6** But without faith it is impossible to please Him, for he who comes to God must believe that He is, and that He is a rewarder of those who diligently seek Him. (NKJV)

**Jeremiah 29:11** For I know the plans I have for you," declares the Lord, "plans to prosper you and not to harm you, plans to give you hope and a future. (NIV)

## Psalms 23

1 The Lord is my shepherd;

I shall not want.

2 He makes me to lie down in green pastures;

He leads me beside the still waters.

3 He restores my soul;

He leads me in the paths of righteousness

For His name's sake.

4 Yea, though I walk through the valley of the shadow of death,

I will fear no evil;

For You are with me;

Your rod and Your staff, they comfort me.

5 You prepare a table before me in the presence of my enemies;

You anoint my head with oil;

My cup runs over.

6 Surely goodness and mercy shall follow me

All the days of my life;

And I will dwell[a] in the house of the Lord

Forever. (NKJV)

**Hebrews 11:1** Now faith is the substance of things hoped for, the evidence of things not seen.

**Hebrews 11:8** By faith Abraham, when he was called to go out into a place which he should after receive for an inheritance, obeyed; and he went out, not knowing whither he went.

9 By faith he sojourned in the land of promise, as in a strange country, dwelling in tabernacles with Isaac and Jacob, the heirs with him of the same promise:

10 For he looked for a city which hath foundations, whose builder and maker is God.

Hebrews 11:3 By faith [that is, with an inherent trust and enduring confidence in the power, wisdom and goodness of God] we understand that the worlds (universe, ages) were framed and created [formed, put in order, and equipped for their intended purpose] by the word of God, so that what is seen was not made out of things which are visible. (AMP)

11 Through faith also Sara herself received strength to conceive seed, and was delivered of a child when she was past age, because she judged him faithful who had promised.

Hebrews 11:20 By faith Isaac blessed Jacob and Esau concerning things to come.

21 By faith Jacob, when he was dying, blessed both the sons of Joseph; and worshipped, leaning upon the top of his staff.

22 By faith Joseph, when he died, made mention of the departing of the children of Israel; and gave commandment concerning his bones.

23 By faith Moses, when he was born, was hid three months of his parents, because they saw he was a proper child; and they were not afraid of the king's commandment.

24 By faith Moses, when he was come to years, refused to be called the son of Pharaoh's daughter;

**Hebrews 11:30** By faith the walls of Jericho fell down, after they were compassed about seven days.

## Psalm 91 Amplified Bible (AMP)

Security of the One Who Trusts in the Lord.

**Psalm 91** He who [a]dwells in the shelter of the Most High

Will remain secure and rest in the shadow of the Almighty [whose power no enemy can withstand].

### 2

I will say of the Lord, "He is my refuge and my fortress,

My God, in whom I trust [with great confidence, and on whom I rely]!"

### 3

For He will save you from the trap of the fowler,

And from the deadly pestilence.

### 4

He will cover you and completely protect you with His pinions,

And under His wings you will find refuge;

His faithfulness is a shield and a wall.

## 5

You will not be afraid of the terror of night,

Nor of the arrow that flies by day,

## 6

Nor of the pestilence that stalks in darkness,

Nor of the destruction (sudden death) that lays waste at noon.

## 7

A thousand may fall at your side

And ten thousand at your right hand,

But danger will not come near you.

## 8

You will only [be a spectator as you] look on with your eyes

And witness the [divine] repayment of the wicked [as you watch safely from the shelter of the Most High].

## 9

Because you have made the Lord, [who is] my refuge,

Even the Most High, your dwelling place,

10

No evil will befall you,

Nor will any plague come near your tent.

11

For He will command His angels in regard to you,

To protect and defend and guard you in all your ways [of obedience and service].

12

They will lift you up in their hands,

So that you do not [even] strike your foot against a stone.

13

You will tread upon the lion and cobra;

The young lion and the serpent you will trample underfoot.

## 14

"Because he set his love on Me, therefore I will save him;

I will set him [securely] on high, because he knows My name [he confidently trusts and relies on Me, knowing I will never abandon him, no, never].

## 15

"He will call upon Me, and I will answer him;

I will be with him in trouble;

I will rescue him and honor him.

## 16

"With a long life I will satisfy him

And I will let him see My salvation."

## Psalm 1 Amplified Bible (AMP)

Book One

The Righteous and the Wicked Contrasted.

### 1

Blessed [fortunate, prosperous, and favored by God] is the man who does not walk in the counsel of the wicked [following their advice and example],

Nor stand in the path of sinners,

Nor sit [down to rest] in the seat of [b]scoffers (ridiculers).

### 2

But his delight is in the law of the Lord,

And on His law [His precepts and teachings] he [habitually] meditates day and night.

### 3

And he will be like a tree firmly planted [and fed] by streams of water,

Which yields its fruit in its season;

Its leaf does not wither;

And in whatever he does, he prospers [and comes to maturity].

4

The wicked [those who live in disobedience to God's law] are not so,

But they are like the chaff [worthless and without substance] which the wind blows away.

5

Therefore the wicked will not stand [unpunished] in the judgment,

Nor sinners in the assembly of the righteous.

6

For the Lord knows and fully approves the way of the righteous,

But the way of the wicked shall perish.

**2 Corinthians 9:6-7** But this I say: He who sows sparingly will also reap sparingly, and he who sows bountifully will also reap bountifully. 7 So let each one give as he purposes in his heart, not grudgingly or of necessity; for God loves a cheerful giver. (NKJV)

**Joshua 1:8** This Book of the Law shall not depart from your mouth, but you shall meditate in it day and night, that you may observe to do according to all that is written in it. For then you will make your way prosperous, and then you will have good success. (NKJV)

**Isaiah 54:17** No weapon formed against you shall prosper, And every tongue which rises against you in judgment You shall condemn. This is the heritage of the servants of the Lord, And their righteousness is from Me," Says the Lord. (NKJV)

**Isaiah 61:7** Instead of your shame you shall have double honor, And instead of confusion they shall rejoice in their portion.  Therefore in their land they shall possess double; Everlasting joy shall be theirs. (NKJV)

**Psalm 37:4** Delight yourself also in the Lord, And He shall give you the desires of your heart. (NKJV)

**Matthew 6:33** But seek first the kingdom of God and His righteousness, and all these things shall be added to you. (NKJV)

**Philippians 4:13** I can do all things through Christ who strengthens me. (NKJV)

**Proverbs 16:3** Commit your works to the Lord, And your thoughts will be established. (NKJV)

**Ephesians 1:15-21** Therefore I also, after I heard of your faith in the Lord Jesus and your love for all the saints, 16 do not cease to give thanks for you, making mention of you in my prayers: 17 that the God of our Lord Jesus Christ, the Father of glory, may give to you the spirit of wisdom and revelation in the knowledge of Him, 18 the eyes of your understanding being enlightened; that you may know what is the hope of His calling, what are the riches of the glory of His inheritance in the saints, 19 and what is the exceeding greatness of His power toward us who believe, according to the working of His mighty power 20 which He worked in Christ when He raised Him from the dead and seated Him at His right hand in the heavenly places, 21 far above all principality and power and might and dominion, and every name that is named, not only in this age but also in that which is to come. (NKJV)

# Resources for Mompreneurs

| Name | Address | Website | Email |
|---|---|---|---|
| It's My Time to Rise Business Institute & Entrepreneurial Center for Women | 1820 Tribute Rd., Ste L, Sacramento, CA 95815 | http://www.itsmytimetorise.com/ | coachsheya@gmail.com |
| Professional Business Women of California | 2977 Ygnacio Valley Rd., Suite 179, Walnut Creek, CA 94598 | http://pbwc.org/ | info@pbwc.org |
| The Founding Moms | 2020 N. California Ave., Ste. 7-204, Chicago, IL 60647 | https://foundingmoms.com/ | jill@foundingmoms.com |
| American Association of University Women | 1331 Garden Highway, Suite 100, Sacramento, CA 95833 | http://www.aauw-ca.org/ | office@aauw-ca.org |
| Mompreneur Show | | http://Mompreneurshow.com/ | http://Mompreneurshow.com/contact/ |
| The BOSS Network | | http://www.thebossnetwork.org/ | info@thebossnetwork.org |
| California Capital | 1792 Tribute Rd. #270, | http://cacapital.org/busi | |

| | | | |
|---|---|---|---|
| Women's Business Center | Sacramento, CA 95815 | ness-assistance/ womens-business-center/ | |
| Lenise Williams Esq. Attorney & Business Consultant) | 3379 Peachtree Rd. NE, Atlanta, GA 30326 | http://www. lenisewilliam s.com/ | info@lenisewi lliams.com |
| Virtual Assistant Onlinejobs. ph | Flowing Air Studios LLC, 770 E Main St. #250, Lehi, UT 84043 | https://ww w.onlinejobs. ph/ | support@Onli neJobs.ph |

# Reference

Score. (2016). Resource. Infographic Women Small Business. Retrieved from,

https://www.score.org/resource/infographic-women-small-business

*Natasha Miller,*

*MS, RHIA, CPC, CPB, CPC-I, AAPC Certified ICD-10-CM Trainer.*

*Speaker, Author, Health Information Educator, Medical Mompreneur, Founder & CEO, Natasha Miller & Associates, LLC & Northern California Medical Billing & Coding Institute*

Natasha Miller is a wife, mother of five, entrepreneur, and speaker. She is the CEO & Founder of Natasha Miller & Associates, LLC, where one of her main responsibilities is to prepare students to pass the Certified Professional Coder (CPC) and Certified Professional Biller (CPB) certification exams. Natasha is involved in her church and community, where she enjoys ministering to youth and adults about visions, dreams, and goals.

Natasha is a leader in health information management and is certified through the American Academy of Professional Coders (AAPC). She is a Registered Health Information Administrator (RHIA) through AHIMA. Natasha holds her Certified Professional Coder (CPC), Certified Professional Biller (CPB), and Certified Professional Coder – Instructor (CPC-I) certifications, and is an AAPC Certified ICD-10-CM Trainer. She has over 18 years of combined professional healthcare experience in medical coding, medical records, clinical, teaching provider documentation, medical insurance eligibility, claims adjudication, supervision, compliance, and auditing.

Natasha received her Master of Science degree in Health Information Management (HIM) from The College of St. Scholastica in

2016. She received her Bachelor of Science degree in Healthcare Management from Walden University in 2012. Natasha received her Associate of Science degree in Social Sciences from Sacramento City College in 2007. She teaches medical coding and medical billing. She has also taught medical billing, coding, and auditing to medical coders in corporate America. Her experiences include project management and consulting. Natasha is also an online adjunct instructor for Health Information Technology, Medical Billing and Coding.

Natasha is a member of the AAPC and AHIMA. She loves to learn and participate in seminars, workshops, and conferences to stay current with health information management and the business of medicine. She has a passion for mentoring new coders and is excited when one of her previous students calls to say that they have passed their certification exam.

Natasha found her first job in the healthcare field in 2000, when she worked at the VA Medical Center in Mather, California as an Information Receptionist in the G.I. Clinic. Natasha has worked as a Medical Biller, Medical Coder, Lead Coder, Trainer, Instructor, and Consultant in this industry. She has worked for large health care organizations and small practices. Natasha has also worked from home as a Medical Coder. She has traveled to and consulted in more than 200 physician offices, where she trained billers, coders, nurses, office managers, and providers. Natasha has worked with the credential organization AAPC and wrote part of the new CPC curriculum for 2016. She enjoys putting on workshops, seminars, and boot camps to help healthcare professionals and students advance in their careers in the medical industry. Natasha imparts the wealth of knowledge she has learned and experienced in the business side of medicine to the clients and students with whom she works.

## Natasha C. Miller

MS, RHIA, CPC, CPC-I, CPB
CEO/ Founder

916-365-2880
info@ncmbci.com
www.ncmbci.com
@NCMBCI
@NCMBCI
@NCMBCI

**Mailing Address:**
8250 Calvine RD C228
Sacramento CA 95828

## Northern California Medical Billing & Coding Institute

## www.ncmbci.com

The Northern California Medical Billing & Coding Institute (NCMBCI) offers short-term medical coding and reimbursement certification classroom programs in the Sacramento and Central Valley areas. It also offers online courses. The population it serves consists of individuals in the healthcare field, displaced workers, semi-retirees, and high school graduates entering the field of medical coding and reimbursement.

NCMBCI is licensed by the American Academy of Professional Coders (AAPC) to facilitate its Professional Medical Coding Curriculum and Professional Medical Billing Curriculum. All instructors are CPC and CPC-I credentialed by the American Academy of Professional Coders. Courses are offered on weeknights and weekends as well as online to accommodate the scheduling needs and child care responsibilities of working professionals. Two- and three-day boot camps and review classes are offered along with workshops and seminars. NCMBCI also provides onsite training in medical coding, billing, and reimbursement. The AAPC Professional Medical Coding Curriculum and Professional Medical Billing Curriculum prepare students for successfully testing for the Certified Professional Coder

(CPC) or Certified Professional Biller (CPB) examinations. Due to the quality of its programs and its instructors' dedication, 95% of its students pass the CPC or CPB examinations. NCMBCI provides consulting services along with baseline, concurrent, and retrospective audits that help practices avoid government and commercial audits.

**Northern California Medical Billing & Coding Institute**

15 Business Park Way Ste 109
Sacramento Ca 95828

Natasha C. Miller Family

Pictured (Arguster, Natasha, Neema, Jacqlyn, Judah, Jaron, & Jadon)

Natasha C. Miller - Speaker

Natasha C. Miller, MS, RHIA, CPC, CPB, CPC-I is a change agent who is able to motivate and inspire healthcare professionals, women, moms, young girls, and anyone seeking to improve themselves.

Natasha is a dynamic speaker who will have you wanting to pursue your passions and goals. Natasha also has in-depth knowledge of health information management and speaks on HIPAA, electronic health records, code sets, and more.

**To book Natasha for your next keynote, workshop, or training, please visit http://www.natashacmiller.com/speaker.html and fill out a short speaker form.**

Natasha is also co-author of *Stand Up Be Heard Volume II*, which you can purchase at http://www.natashacmiller.com/products.html